A Beginning-to-Read Book

Fourth of July

by Mary Lindeen

NORWOOD HOUSE PRESS

DEAR CAREGIVER, The *Beginning to Read—Read and Discover* books provide emergent readers the opportunity to explore the world through nonfiction while building early reading skills. The text integrates both common sight words and content vocabulary. These key words are featured on lists provided at the back of the book to help your child expand his or her sight word recognition, which helps build reading fluency. The content words expand vocabulary and support comprehension.

Nonfiction text is any text that is factual. The Common Core State Standards call for an increase in the amount of informational text reading among students. The Standards aim to promote college and career readiness among students. Preparation for college and career endeavors requires proficiency in reading complex informational texts in a variety of content areas. You can help your child build a foundation by introducing nonfiction early. To further support the CCSS, you will find Reading Reinforcement activities at the back of the book that are aligned to these Standards.

Above all, the most important part of the reading experience is to have fun and enjoy it!

Sincerely,

Shannon Cannon

Shannon Cannon, Ph.D.
Literacy Consultant

Norwood House Press • P.O. Box 316598 • Chicago, Illinois 60631
For more information about Norwood House Press please visit our website at
www.norwoodhousepress.com or call 866-565-2900.
© 2019 Norwood House Press. Beginning-to-Read™ is a trademark of Norwood House Press.
All rights reserved. No part of this book may be reproduced or utilized in any form or by any
means without written permission from the publisher.

Editor: Judy Kentor Schmauss
Designer: Lindaanne Donohoe

Photo Credits:
Shutterstock, cover, 1, 6-7, 12-13; iStock Photo, 3, 4-5, 8-9, 10-11, 14-15,
16-17, 18-19, 20-21, 22-23, 24-25, 26-27, 28-29

Library of Congress Cataloging-in-Publication Data
Names: Lindeen, Mary, author.
Title: Fourth of July / by Mary Lindeen.
Description: Chicago, IL : Norwood House Press, 2018. | "A Beginning to Read
  Book."
Identifiers: LCCN 2018004462 (print) | LCCN 2018020027 (ebook) | ISBN
  9781684041749 (eBook) | ISBN 9781599539096 (library edition : alk. paper)
Subjects: LCSH: Fourth of July celebrations-Juvenile literature. | Fourth of
  July-Juvenile literature.
Classification: LCC E286 (ebook) | LCC E286 .A13936 2018 (print) | DDC
  394.2634-dc23
LC record available at https://lccn.loc.gov/2018004462

Hardcover ISBN: 978-1-59953-909-6   Paperback ISBN: 978-1-68404-165-7

312N-072018
Manufactured in the United States of America in North Mankato, Minnesota.

The Fourth of July is a summer holiday.

It is always on the same date in July.

You will see lots of red, white, and blue on the Fourth of July.

Red, white, and
blue are the colors
of our flag.

You will see flags
in lots of places.

You will see flags
on houses.

You will see flags
in parades.

You will even see
flags on bikes!

You can have fun on the Fourth of July.

You can go to a park.

You can have a picnic.

You can go swimming.

You can eat red,
white, and blue
treats!

When it gets dark,
the fun doesn't end.

You can watch
fireworks!

They light up the
night sky.

The Fourth of July is a day of flags, food, and fun!

Happy Fourth of July!

CRAFT AND STRUCTURE

To check your child's understanding of the organization of the book, recreate the following chart on a sheet of paper. Read the book with your child, and then help him or her fill in the diagram using what they learned. Work together to complete the chart by writing words or ideas from the book that answer the questions:

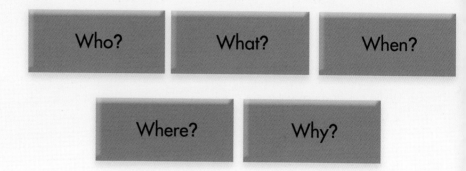

Who?   What?   When?

Where?   Why?

VOCABULARY: Learning Content Words

Content words are words that are specific to a particular topic. All of the content words for this book can be found on page 32. Use some or all of these content words to complete one or more of the following activities:

- Give 4-5 clues about each word to your child and have him or her guess the word.

- Have your child act out the words.

- Write the words and their definitions on different pieces of paper. Turn them face down and play Concentration.

- Help your child make associations between two content words. Pick any two content words, and have your child think of something these two words have in common.

- Have your child find smaller words or word parts within words.

FOUNDATIONAL SKILLS: *r*-Controlled Vowels

An *r*-controlled vowel is a vowel (*a, e, i, o, u*) followed by the letter r; for example, the letter *a* is an *r*-controlled vowel in *car*. In *car*, *a* and *r* blend together to make the sound /ar/. Have your child say the words with *r*-controlled vowels in the list below. Then help your child find other words with *r*-controlled vowels in this book.

summer	are	yard
color	parades	park
dark	fireworks	your

CLOSE READING OF INFORMATIONAL TEXT

Close reading helps children comprehend text. It includes reading a text, discussing it with others, and answering questions about it. Use these questions to discuss this book with your child.

- Where are two places you can find flags on the Fourth of July?

- Why do we see so many red, white, and blue things on the Fourth of July?

- How is the Fourth of July like other holidays? How is it different?

- What's a picnic? Why might the Fourth of July be a good time to have one?

- How does your family celebrate the Fourth of July?

- What would happen if you tried to watch fireworks during the day?

FLUENCY

Fluency is the ability to read accurately with speed and expression. Help your child practice fluency by using one or more of the following activities:

- Reread this book to your child at least two times while he or she uses a finger to track each word as it is read.

- Read the first sentence aloud. Then have your child reread the sentence with you. Continue until you have finished the book.

- Ask your child to read aloud the words they know on each page of this book. (Your child will learn additional words with subsequent readings.)

- Have your child practice reading this book several times to improve accuracy, rate, and expression.

··· Word List ···

Fourth of July uses the 56 words listed below. *High-frequency words* are those words that are used most often in the English language. They are sometimes referred to as sight words because children need to learn to recognize them automatically when they read. *Content words* are any words specific to a particular topic. Regular practice reading these words will enhance your child's ability to read with greater fluency and comprehension.

High-Frequency Words

a	eat	in	red	when
always	end	is	same	white
and	even	it	see	will
are	get(s)	of	the	you
blue	go	on	they	
can	have	our	to	
day	house(s)	place(s)	up	

Content Words

bikes	fireworks	happy	night	summer
colors	flag(s)	holiday	parades	swimming
dark	food	July	park	treats
date	Fourth	light	picnic	watch
doesn't	fun	lots	sky	

··· About the Author

Mary Lindeen is a writer, editor, parent, and former elementary school teacher. She has written more than 100 books for children and edited many more. She specializes in early literacy instruction and books for young readers, especially nonfiction.

··· About the Advisor

Dr. Shannon Cannon is an elementary school teacher in Sacramento, California. She has served as a teacher educator in the School of Education at UC Davis, where she also earned her Ph.D. in Language, Literacy, and Culture. As a member of the clinical faculty, she supervised pre-service teachers and taught elementary methods courses in reading, effective teaching, and teacher action research.